SO-CMR-939

CANOPY
B O O K S

Printed in the USA

ISBN: 978-1-946426-37-6

Contents

Be a Good Joker

Do you love to prank your friends and family? If so, this book is for you! In these pages, you'll find instructions for tons of hilarious practical jokes.

Pranking people is only fun if you do it right. However, poorly thought-out pranks can be mean and upsetting—or can get you in trouble. Follow these "golden rules of pranking" to keep your pranks in the funny zone.

1. A prank should be funny. Victim will laugh: GOOD. Victim will be upset: BAD.

2. A prank should never cause permanent damage to property.

3. A prank should never hurt or make fun of anyone.

4. You must clean up all messy pranks afterward. It's unfair to make the victim do it.

5. Don't pull any prank that involves something that you know your parents would not allow.

6. You should know your victims. It's not cool to prank strangers.

7. Be a good sport. Don't get upset if your victims prank you back. Just laugh…and start planning your next attack!

Wacky Water Tricks

These silly soaking tricks are sure to have you drowning in laughter!

WET HANDSHAKE!

1. After you're done using the bathroom, wet a paper towel or a wad of toilet paper. Make sure it's not too big to fit in your hand.

2. Hide the wet paper in your hand—give it a squeeze if it's so wet that it's dripping.

3. Offer to shake the hand of the first person you see—you can say something like "You did a great job today" to have a reason for the handshake.

4. Watch as your target jumps back and pulls away when they think they've gotten a handful of something horrible!

CAUGHT A BUG!

This is the perfect prank to pull after dinner while the whole family is cleaning up—there will be lots of targets available!

1. While washing your hands or doing the dishes, discreetly fill your hands with water.

2. Tell a friend or family member that you caught a bug in the sink! Hold out your cupped hands.

3. When the victim bends down to take a look, squeeze your palms together quickly and firmly. Water will shoot out of your hands—straight at your victim!

SOMETHING IN THE WATER

1. Offer to pour a glass of water for your target. A perfect time would be right before dinner—offer to pour a glass for each member of your family. Or you can offer a glass to a friend who is visiting.

2. Sneakily add a small amount of either sugar or salt to the glass. Use just a tiny bit. Give it a stir so it dissolves completely.

3. The water won't taste terrible, but it will just seem a little bit "off." See how long your friends complain before they give up on their oh-so-slightly-seasoned drinks.

KEEP IT GOING!: Pour a glass for yourself too, but don't put anything in it—when your target remarks on the way the water tastes, you can say, "Tastes fine to me!" and offer a sip from your glass. They might say yours tastes different—try theirs and say, "They taste the same!" Your victim will think their taste buds are malfunctioning!

CUP TRAP

1. Fill two plastic cups with water.
2. Challenge a friend to balance one cup on the back of each hand. (This works best if the friend places both hands palm down on a table.)
3. When the full cups are in place, refuse to move them. Unless your friend figures out how to pick up the cups by biting them, they won't get loose without getting wet!

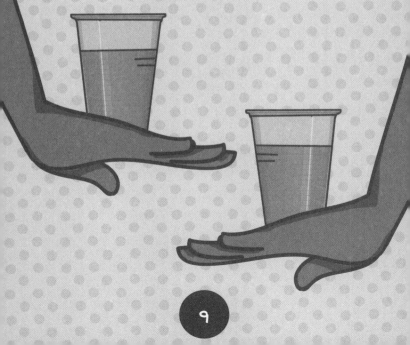

UPSIDE-DOWN CUPS

1. Grab a clear cup. The hard plastic kind works great if you have it.

2. Add about two inches of water and two ice cubes to the cup.

3. Cut out a thin piece of cardboard that's slightly larger than the cup. (A cereal box works great for this!)

4. Place the cardboard on top of the cup.

5. Make sure you've secured the cardboard all the way around the top of the cup, and carefully turn the cup upside down. The water should help the cardboard stick. (Make sure you have towels handy!)

6. Place the cup down on the bathroom sink, keeping the cardboard underneath.

7. Hold on to the cup and slide it off the cardboard and onto the counter. Some people like to slide quickly and some people like to slide slowly. This part takes practice, so do some test runs before you try to prank someone!

8. Wipe up any water on the counter.

9. Add a sign that says "Have fun cleaning this up!"

Pro Tip

To empty the cup, just slide it over to the sink basin and let the water go down the drain.

Bonkers Bathroom

Everyone uses the bathroom several times a day. Make these visits memorable with these funny pranks. Grab some clear tape for the first three tricks!

TOOTHPASTE TROUBLE

1. Sneak into the bathroom before your target is going to brush their teeth. (Make sure to brush yours first if you need to!)

2. Carefully put clear tape over the mouth of someone's toothpaste tube. Trim any extra with scissors so that it is as hidden as possible. Replace the cap and wait for your target.

3. With a little luck, your victim won't notice the tape when they unscrew the cap. They'll squeeze harder and harder trying to get the toothpaste out. Sooner or later, there will be a toothpaste eruption as the tape gives way!

SPOUT OFF

You should get a parent's permission before performing this prank.

1. Use tape to mostly block the mouth of a bathroom or kitchen faucet. Leave just a small opening near the front.

2. Turn on the tap *slowly* to test that the tape will hold and that it is coming out in the direction you want. If you turn it on too fast—you're likely to get wet and then the joke will be on you!

3. Wait nearby for someone to use the sink. When someone turns on the tap, water will blast straight outward. Will it soak your victim's pants, shirt, or face? It depends on the tape's exact position. You'll just have to wait and see!

ALL ROLLED UP

1. Grab some clear tape and measure off a piece that is exactly the same width as a roll of toilet paper.

2. Locate the end of the toilet paper roll. Carefully place the piece of tape along the edge of the last piece, so that you are taping it to the rest of the roll.

3. Turn the roll so the tape is not visible.

4. Wait for someone to use the bathroom—when they try to tear off a piece of toilet paper, they won't be able to!

TOILET PAPER TELEGRAM

1. Grab a marker or pen and head into the bathroom.

2. Take the toilet paper off the holder. Unroll at least ten sheets, or more if you like.

3. Write on one sheet "Help! I'm trapped in a toilet paper factory!" If you're using marker, make sure it's dry before the next step.

4. Carefully reroll the toilet paper and place it back on the holder. Someone will find the funny message when they use the toilet paper!

15

MESSAGE IN THE MIRROR

Here's a perfect prank if you have a sibling who takes really long, hot showers.

1. Before your target is going to use the shower, use your finger to write a creepy message on the bathroom mirror, like "Beware the ghost" or "I arrive at midnight." You won't be able to see anything, so be precise!

2. Wait for your target to take a shower. As they are showering, steam will fog up the mirror—except for where you wrote your message. The oils from your finger will keep the steam from settling on those spots, and the message will appear.

3. Listen for the scream as your target gets out of the shower and notices the spooky sentence! EEK!

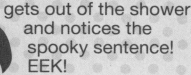

SUDLESS SOAP

This trick is going to render a bar of soap completely useless, so make sure to get a parent's permission before performing this prank.

1. Get a completely dry bar of soap. If it's brand-new, great—if not, dry with paper towels and then let it air-dry completely before the next step.

2. Cover the soap with clear fingernail polish. Let the polish dry, then put the soap in the shower or by the sink.

3. The next person who tries to use the soap will be frustrated when no suds appear!

WHEN YOU GOTTA GO...

It may not be Halloween (or maybe it is!), but you can still mummy-fy your toilet to make things difficult for someone who's gotta go!

1. Ask your parents if you can use an extra roll of toilet paper for this prank (and warn them about what will happen to their bathroom!).

2. Tape the end of the toilet paper to the underside of the toilet seat.

3. Start circling the toilet seat with the toilet paper so that the toilet paper covers the whole seat, including the hole in the middle.

4. Once the hole is covered, tape the end of the toilet paper to the underside of the toilet seat and close the lid so the paper isn't visible when you enter the room.

5. When your friend comes over, make sure to keep their water glass filled so they really have to go to the bathroom. Then wait for them to react when they enter the bathroom. And then, of course, be a really good friend and help them clear away the toilet paper so they can finally use the toilet.

Funny Food

Turn mealtime into comedy hour with these silly and easy pranks.

SAVORY SUNDAE

Make a dinnertime "sundae" using mashed potatoes and gravy, arranged artfully in a see-through sundae dish. Put a cherry on top to complete the illusion. You might not fool anyone, but you'll definitely make them smile!

"SPONGE" CAKE

Everyone likes sponge cake…but not this kind! Take at least one real sponge or, even better, several sponges. (You can get packs of cheap sponges at any dollar store, if you don't have them around your house.) Arrange the sponges in a stack. Cover them with real frosting or whipped cream, and then place your delicious-looking creation on the table. Your dinner companions will get quite a shock when they cut into this deceptive dessert!

POP! TART

For a variation on the cake theme, blow up a balloon and frost it. Present it to your unsuspecting target as a delicious dessert, telling them you would like them to cut the first piece. When they go to take a slice—POP!

SWEET SURPRISE

This prank is an oldie but a goodie. Dump all of the salt in the saltshaker into a resealable bag or container and hide it in the cupboard. Refill the saltshaker with sugar. Your family is in for a sweet surprise!

COLD CEREAL

Fool your siblings with a bowl of frozen cereal!

1. Put some cereal into a bowl, add milk, and freeze overnight.

2. In the morning, place the bowl on the table. Pour just enough fresh milk into the bowl to cover the frozen milk.

3. Tell your sibling you got their cereal for them. Watch the confusion when they try—and fail—to dip their spoon into their rock-hard breakfast!

HEALTHY HOAX

This prank takes some time and effort, but it's worth it!

1. Carefully pull open the bottoms of several snack-size bags of chips.

2. Remove the chips and save them in a resealable baggie.

3. Place carrots or celery into the now-empty chip bags.

4. Tape the bags shut, and then serve the "chips" to your friends. Sit back and wait for the groans to begin!

GUMMY WORM SANDWICH

This prank seems sickening, but it's really sweet!

1. Offer to make a sandwich for a friend or family member. (You can say you're going to make one for yourself and ask if they would like one, to make it seem more believable.)

2. When you are making the sandwich, sneak a couple gummy worms inside.

3. Watch as your target takes their first bite and finds something they didn't expect! They might think it's a real worm at first— but they won't be grossed out when they realize it's just candy.

Pro Tip

This trick is best to do with a peanut butter and jelly sandwich— it will still taste good, so you won't be wasting any ingredients!

AN EGG-CELLENT PRANK

**This is a great early morning prank—
but you might want to
set it up the night before!**

1. Grab a bunch of googly eyes from the craft store.

2. Glue a pair of googly eyes on each egg in the fridge.

3. Ask your parents to make you an omelet for breakfast.

4. When they open the carton, they'll certainly be surprised to see all the eggs looking at them!

Pro Tip

If you want to get fancy, you can grab a marker and draw the rest of each egg's face!

Comedic Confusion

These pranks are meant to confuse your victims, not startle them. See how long you can keep up these funny jokes before people catch on!

SILLY SIGN

Use a dark marker to write "Honk and Wave!" on a piece of paper. Secretly tape the sign to the back of your parents' car right before you leave the house. You're guaranteed to get lots of friendly attention on your drive…much to the driver's confusion!

FUNNY FACE

Tell a friend that they have a booger in their nose. Giggle while the friend discreetly tries to solve the problem. When they're done, tell the friend that the booger is still there. Repeat until your friend figures out you're pulling their leg…or, in this case, their nose!

SHRINKING SHOES

Stuff a little bit of cotton wool into the toes of a sibling's sneakers. Just a little! When your sibling puts the shoes on, they'll feel a little too tight. Repeat this process each day so the shoes get tighter and tighter. Count the days until your prank is discovered!

BAFFLING BIRTHDAY

Tell everyone that it's your BFF's birthday (even though it isn't). Your buddy will be bewildered when they receive birthday greetings all day long!

WORTH THE WEIGHT

This prank could go on for a long time, if you're careful and lucky.

1. Gather a bunch of small rocks and stones. Put in a bag and bring it to school—stash it in your locker, backpack, or desk.

2. Every day, sneak one small rock into a friend's backpack. As the backpack gets heavier and heavier, your friend will start to complain, much to your amusement.

3. Keep it up! Make sure to spread out where you are placing the rocks so they won't be noticed—put in different pockets or pouches inside the backpack.

4. When they finally figure it out, weigh the rocks to see exactly how extreme your prank became!

ALMOST FAMOUS

Your friend will never guess who's calling! If you don't have a cell phone, your parents can help you with this prank.

1. Change a friend's name in your cell phone to the name of your target's celebrity crush.

2. Ask your friend to call you at a time you know you will be hanging out with your target.

3. On your phone, it will look like the celebrity is calling you directly!

4. Have a phone conversation planned out with your friend to make the call seem natural. Like, "Oh yeah, Taylor, you really crushed that performance. It was so nice to meet you last week!"

5. Don't laugh!

6. Make sure the target sees the name on your phone and realizes who you say you're talking to.

7. If they say they doesn't believe you, hand over your phone and tell them to call the celeb themselves. They'll be in for a surprise when they hear a real voice at the other end of the line! You can go even further by having a clip of the celebrity ready to play on the other end of the phone.

BACKWARDS DAY

You can play this prank any day of the year, but it works especially well the day after a sleepover.

1. When you wake up, put on all your clothes backwards—your shirt, your pants, your hat, everything. If you go outside, put your coat on backwards.

2. Act as normally as possible. Don't mention anything about your clothes. If someone says something to you, act as if they're weird, not you.

3. If you have a couple of friends over, you can do this by yourself and try to convince them that nothing's wrong.

PRANKING: FAMILY-STYLE

You know who hates getting up in the morning? Teenagers. This is an especially good prank to play on a teenage sibling. But it'll work on anyone! Get your parents to help play along and pull this one off.

1. Pick a Saturday and convince a sibling that Saturday is actually a school day. Hide all the calendars so they don't find out what day it really is!

2. Make sure everyone sets their alarms and does exactly what they would do on a school day: get dressed, make breakfast, pack backpacks, make lunches…the works!

3. Either set your sibling's alarm, or make sure they wake up the same way they normally do on a school day.

4. You can really make them nervous if one of your parents says that you're late! Rush around even faster than normal.

5. If you can keep up the prank, don't tell your sibling until you're all actually out the door. If you can, have everyone shout, "GOTCHA!" together.

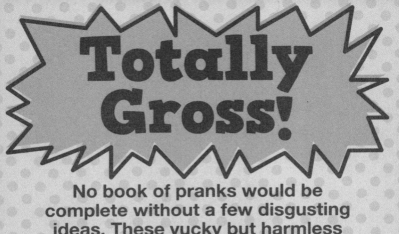

Totally Gross!

No book of pranks would be complete without a few disgusting ideas. These yucky but harmless jokes are sure to get groans from your victims!

SLOPPY SNEEZE

We sneeze when stuff gets in our nose that shouldn't be there. Sneezing blasts that stuff out of our bodies. But how can you fake a sneeze? Follow these steps:

1. Wet a small piece of paper towel and hide it in your hand *(or see the MYO snot activity on page 39 and use a little bit of that for this prank).*

2. Squint your eyes and scrunch up your nose like it itches.

3. Take a few fast, deep breaths without making a sound.

4. Take a final deep breath and bring your hands up to your face.

5. Let out a big "CHOO!" sound, and quickly flick the wet paper towel in the direction you want it to go.

6. Sniffle, and rub your nose to complete the act, keeping a lookout to see if the "booger" hit your target.

Pro Tip

Saying just "CHOO!" instead of "AHH-CHOO!" sounds more like a real sneeze.

If you want to learn how to make yourself give an honest-to-goodness real sneeze, you can try:

- **Tickling your nose with the edge of a tissue**
- **Running your tongue up and down the roof of your mouth**
- **Smelling strong perfume**

SCRATCHY SCALP

Here's another great "illness" to spring on your friends.

1. Secretly sprinkle a bunch of salt into your hair.

2. When you see your buddies, start scratching your scalp like crazy. "Will you take a look at my head?" you say.

3. Your friends will be horrified to see that you have the worst dandruff EVER. Revolting!!

Pro Tip Try this trick by sprinkling black pepper into your hair instead of salt—ew! Lice!

HORRIBLE HUG

1. Put on some workout or gym clothes.
2. Use water to dampen your T-shirt, face, and hair to look like you're sweating madly.
3. Go up to a friend and give them a big, damp, "sweaty" hug. Chuckle as they recoil in horror!

BUG OUT!

1. At lunchtime, hide a raisin in a napkin.
2. Pretend to squash an imaginary bug, and then pick it up with the napkin.
3. Quickly pluck out the raisin. Before anyone has time to see what it really is, throw the raisin at a friend… then enjoy their wiggling, jiggling "getaway" dance!

Pro Tip

To make this trick extra gross, eat the raisin instead of throwing it!

BLOODY BLUFF!

Make your own fake blood to pull some gory gags.

1. In a resealable container with a lid, mix 5 tablespoons (74 ml) of light corn syrup, 1/2 teaspoon (2.5 ml) of red food coloring, 1 drop of blue food coloring, and 4 to 5 drops of dish soap.

2. Dab the mixture onto your skin to create fake wounds.

3. Walk up to your friends, looking dazed, and wait for them to notice the blood. They'll flip and you'll have the last laugh!

Pro Tip

The recipe makes a good amount so you'll have plenty of fake blood to pull lots of pranks.

FORGOTTEN FLUSH

**Speaking of revolting,
here's another goodie.**

1. With a grown-up's help, carefully remove the lid of your toilet's holding tank.

2. Put 10 drops of yellow food coloring into the water and replace the lid.

3. When the next person to use the bathroom flushes the toilet, the colored water from the holding tank will rush in to fill the toilet bowl. You know the water is fresh— but it sure doesn't look like that way to your victim. "Hey! I thought I flushed that!"

PET PUKE

If you have a pet, mix a little kibble with some white glue. Pour the mixture onto a piece of wax paper. Let it dry completely (this may take a couple of days). When it is dry, trim the edges of the paper. Then set the fake barf on the floor where someone is sure to find it. BAD DOG!

SICKENING SNACK

This prank is super gross for your friends, but delicious for you. Secretly shape a brownie into a piece of fake dog poop. When your friends are watching, pick up the "poop" and eat it. Wait for the howls of disgust to begin!

INSECT ICE

**This is a classic prank
that never gets old.**

1. Find some small plastic bugs. (Little ants or flies are ideal.)

2. Fill an ice cube tray with water, then drop one bug into each compartment.

3. Pop the tray into the freezer until the water hardens.

4. Put the buggy ice cubes into your friends' drinks and wait for the shrieks!

Make sure no one swallows the plastic bug or eats the ice with the bug still in it!

SILLY SNOT

Make your own fake snot to gross out your victims!

1. In a resealable container with a lid, mix together 1/4 cup (4 oz.) white glue and 1/4 cup water.
2. Add 2 to 3 drops of yellow or green food coloring and stir.
3. Add 1/4 cup liquid starch and mix well.
4. Keep the lid on to store your snot!

Prank your friends by hiding some fake snot in your hands and faking a sneeze. Or place a little bit on something of theirs—a glass, their cell phone, their hand. Just don't place it on fabric or an item that might stain.

Funny Money

You may have heard the phrase "funny money." Well, money really IS funny when you use it to play practical jokes on your pals. Grab a few coins and a couple of bucks, and then try the tricks on this page. They're truly priceless!

GONE FISHING

Turn greed into giggles with this hilarious prank.

1. Tape a piece of clear fishing line to a one-dollar bill.

2. Lay the bill on the ground where someone is sure to see it.

3. You hide nearby, keeping a firm grip on the fishing line.

4. When someone tries to pick up the dollar, yank on the fishing line. Try to do it lightly so it seems like it's just the wind moving the dollar.

5. Keep pulling on the bill until your target gives up grabbing!

UNLUCKY PENNY

Here's another trap for the greedy.

1. Use double-stick tape or sticky putty to stick a few coins to a sidewalk.

2. When the coins are firmly stuck, hide nearby and wait for your victims to arrive.

3. Watch as your targets try—and fail—to pick up the coins. There's no telling how many people you'll fool, or how many belly laughs you'll get!

DOLLAR DISGUISE

**Do you want to be rich?
Make your wish come true with
this simple prank!**

1. Cut at least 20 pieces of paper the exact size of a dollar bill.

2. Stack the pieces together, and then put an actual dollar bill on top of the stack.

3. Fold the stack in half with the real dollar on the outside.

4. Watch your friends' jaws drop when you whip out your giant cash stash.

ON THE NOSE

**Here's one more prank that will leave
your victims feeling mighty foolish.**

1. Use a pencil to trace around the edge of a quarter several times. This will leave a thick line of graphite on the coin.

2. Challenge an unsuspecting friend to roll the quarter down their nose. The quarter will leave a black line on your buddy's face. Don't say a word about the mess, of course. Just chuckle whenever you see your streaky pal!

Befuddling Bedroom

The day may be over, but the practical joke fun doesn't have to end quite yet. Bedtime is the perfect time to prank your family. Here are two easy ways to get 'em one last time before they slip off to dreamland!

Fill someone's pillowcase with old candy wrappers or chip bags. Every time your victim moves their head, the wrappers will go "crunch." How annoying!

Sneak into a sibling's bedroom. Adjust all of the clocks in the room one hour forward. In other words, if the actual time is 5 p.m., change the clocks to 6 p.m. If you're lucky, your sibling won't notice. They may go to bed an hour early or even get up an hour early the next morning. Score one for you!

SOCK IT TO 'EM!

This is a great prank to play on a sibling who has all kinds of colorful socks.

1. Take all the socks out of your target's drawer.

2. Make mismatched pairs so that each sock is next to a sock that looks totally different. Keep one pair of matching socks with you.

3. Roll the socks in a ball so that only one color or pattern is visible on the outside of the ball.

4. Place the socks back in the drawer. Your target will likely get angry as they realize that all the socks are mismatched. Before they get too angry, hand them the one pair of matching socks that you saved.

Pro Tip

You can take things a step further and add a little "GOTCHA!" note inside each sock ball!

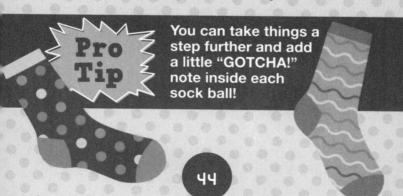

MUSICAL DRAWERS

Ask one of your parents to help you play this hilarious prank on a sibling.

1. Wait until your sibling leaves the house for a few hours, and sneak into their room.

2. Together with a parent, pull out a few of the drawers from their dresser and lay them on the floor. The drawers should all be the same size.

3. Put the drawers back in the dresser—but put them each in a different spot than they were in before. If the sock drawer was at the top, move it to the bottom. If the pants drawer was at the bottom, move it to the middle. Don't touch any of the clothes—move the drawers only.

4. Wait. The waiting might be painful because your sibling might not need to open a drawer until the morning. But wait!

5. The next morning, wake up a little early and keep your ears open for your sibling's screams when they try to find an outfit to wear. Be ready for your sibling to prank you back!

MONSTER UNDER THE BED

1. Grab a cardboard container, like a toilet paper roll, a paper towel roll, or a small cereal box. You'll also need a glow stick or flashlight.

2. Draw a pair of scary-shaped eyes on the cardboard!

3. Cut out the eyes.

4. Put your glow stick or flashlight inside the cardboard so that the holes you cut look like they're glowing. You might have to attach the glow stick or flashlight to the cardboard with masking tape to make it more secure.

5. Hide your glowing monster in a dark place—like in a closet or under the bed— where your target will be sure to find it!

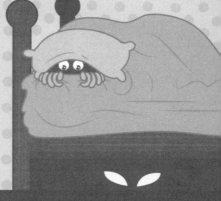

I'M RUBBER AND YOU'RE GLUE...

Does your friend have a prized possession? Make it disappear! (For now...)

1. Identify something small that your friend would realize is missing. It could be a pen or a necklace or a key chain.

2. Sneak that item away from your friend without them noticing. This might be tricky! Ask another friend for help if you need it.

3. Put the item in a small box, like a crayon box or a pencil case. Grab a pile of rubber bands and twist each rubber band around the box, one at a time. You can use as few as 10 rubber bands (to make it a little bit annoying for your friend to get to their stuff) or you can use a whole bag of rubber bands (to make it really annoying to get to their stuff!).

4. Sneak the item back to the place you found it. You can add a little note that says something like:

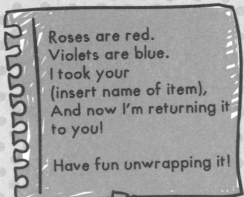

Roses are red.
Violets are blue.
I took your
(insert name of item),
And now I'm returning it
to you!

Have fun unwrapping it!

Or the note can just say:

Ohhhhhh, snap!

Bet you didn't think you'd find your (insert name of item) covered in rubber bands, did you?

Prankfully yours,
Me

Pro Tip

Make sure the item you use for the prank isn't something valuable or irreplaceable.

THAT'S A WRAP!

This is a great prank to play right after December when there's a lot of wrapping paper in the house. It'll be a lot easier with an extra person helping you.

1. When your friend comes over to visit, ask your helper to keep them busy while you work.

2. Grab your friend's backpack and put everything inside on the floor. Wrap each and every item, one by one. Wrap notebooks, textbooks, pens, packs of gum, water bottles, everything.

3. If possible, put everything back where it was and place the backpack exactly where your friend left it. Wait for him to discover their bag full of "presents"!

Pro Tip

This is also a great trick to play on a sibling—or on your whole family. Instead of just wrapping everything inside a backpack, you can wrap every book on a bookshelf!

A PRANK TO SQUEAK ABOUT

Know someone who loooooooves their computer? This is the perfect prank!

1. Print out a picture of you, and use a pen or marker to add a speech bubble that says "GOTCHA!"

2. Grab your target's mouse (the computer kind, not the live animal kind), and turn it upside down.

3. Find the little light. That light tells the mouse where to move on the computer. Once you block it, the mouse won't work.

4. Cover the hole with your photo and use clear tape to attach the photo to the mouse. Make sure you can't see the picture or the tape when the mouse is sitting on the desk.

5. Wait for your target to complain that the mouse doesn't work the next time they try to use it!

TAPE TRICKS

Clear tape is a prankster's best friend. You already saw how you can use it to pull great gags in the bathroom. Grab it again for these funny tricks.

- Put a small piece of tape over the sensor light on your TV remote control. This will stop the remote from working. Let the joke ride while your annoyed victim shakes the remote and changes its batteries. If someone goes to call the cable company for a replacement, though, the joke has gone too far—it's time to spill the beans!

- Use tape to fix light switches in a permanent "on" or "off" position. Unlike the previous two pranks, this one is very easy to detect, so use LOTS of tape. Your victim will have to remove it all before the switch will work. *grumble, grumble*

BUBBLE TROUBLE

1. Start saving bubble wrap.

2. If you have a piece big enough, cut to the size of a bathroom rug or a small rug in your sibling's room.

3. Place the bubble wrap under the rug. You might want to tape it in place so it doesn't show or slide out.

4. It will pop loudly when someone steps onto the rug. This prank is especially effective if you do it first thing in the morning, when your victims are half asleep!

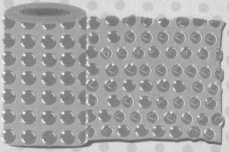

Pro Tip

Try adding a piece of bubble wrap to a family member's pillowcase before bed. They'll get a loud surprise when they go to rest their head!

SHORT SHEET

For the ultimate bedroom prank, try short-sheeting someone's bed.

1. Tuck the top sheet in at the head of the bed instead of the foot.

2. Fold the sheet in half, bringing the untucked end back up to the head of the bed.

3. Add a blanket and pillows to finish the job. The bed now looks perfectly normal but it's not. When someone tries to slip between the sheets, their feet will get stuck partway down the bed. It's the ideal way to end a prank-filled day!

IT'S A PRANK PARTY!

Now that you've learned a ton of great gags, why not gather all your friends for a prank party!

Put all of your prank-loving friends' names in a hat. Everyone can pull one name out of the hat. That is the person you'll play a prank on.

This party needs a few guidelines, so review our rules on (page 5), and make sure to add any of your own prank rules, like:

- Pranks can only happen after school.
- Wait to play your prank until someone pranks you first.
- All pranks should be played on the same day.
- All pranks should happen in the next seven days (Prank Week!).
- Or anything you want!

Decide on your prank rules together, and then keep both eyes open. You never know when your next prank is just around the corner!

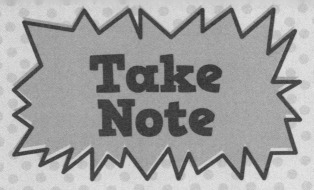

Take Note

You're down to the last prank of the book, but it's a good one! Use the fake notices that came with this book to give your friends and family a shock. There are five different designs, with four copies of each—so you can try each notice a bunch of times. Read on for some ideas.

Pick the perfect victim, time, and place for each notice:

- **Fake money:** Leave one lying outdoors, on the school floor, in someone's wallet—watch your victim get excited—until they realize they've been pranked!

- **City Notice of Extermination:** Tape to a house or bedroom door, or in your classroom or a friend's desk!

- **Overdue Notice:** Deliver to a friend or slip into their library book.

- **Detention Notice:** Leave in a friend's locker or on their desk.

- **Failing Alert:** Leave with friends any time for a sudden shock!

Use the lines on the back side of each notice to let your victim know they've been pranked! You can write a note that says "Just kidding! You've been pranked by (insert your name)!" or write whatever you think is funny!

Cut out each fake notice along the dashed lines printed on the page.

Pro Tip

For extra effect, match each fake notice to a victim's real-life situation. Has a friend broken a school rule and thought they got away with it? DETENTION NOTICE! Is your buddy constantly late with the library books? OVERDUE NOTICE! Is your sister freaking out about finding a spider in her room? CITY NOTICE OF EXTERMINATION! You get the drill. Put your pranking genius to work when delivering these notes. When you run out of notes, take it a step further and make up your own fake notes. How creative can you get? Your imagination is the only limit!

STUDENT DISCIPLINE REFERRAL

 DETENTION

Description of infraction:

Report to the detention hall this afternoon.

OVERDUE NOTICE

Our records show that your books are overdue.

- - - - - - - - - - - - - - - - - - -

Return all checked-out
materials to the library
immediately to avoid a
hefty fine.

LIBRARY

You've Been Pranked!

_____

_____

_____

_____

_____

_____

SCHOOL NOTICE

FAILING ALERT

If you have received this notice, your grade in the following class:

_____

_____ has fallen to failing levels.

Please see your teacher immediately.

You've Been Pranked!

_____

_____

_____

_____

_____

_____

CITY NOTICE

An infestation of insects was found in this room. Extermination was applied. Watch for remaining bugs, especially around the bed.

_____

_____

_____

_____

_____

_____

STUDENT DISCIPLINE REFERRAL

☑ DETENTION

Description of infraction:

Report to the detention hall this afternoon.

_____

_____

_____

_____

_____

_____

OVERDUE NOTICE

Our records show that your books are overdue.

Return all checked-out
materials to the library
immediately to avoid a
hefty fine.

LIBRARY

❦SCHOOL NOTICE❦

FAILING ALERT

If you have received this notice, your grade in the following class:

_____

_____ *has fallen to failing levels.*

Please see your teacher immediately.

CITY NOTICE

An infestation of insects was found in this room. Extermination was applied. Watch for remaining bugs, especially around the bed.

_____

_____

_____

_____

_____

_____

STUDENT DISCIPLINE REFERRAL

 **DETENTION**

Description of infraction:

Report to the detention hall this afternoon.

You've Been Pranked!

_____

_____

_____

_____

_____

_____

OVERDUE NOTICE

Our records show that your books are overdue.

- - - - - - - - - - - - -

Return all checked-out
materials to the library
immediately to avoid a
hefty fine.

LIBRARY

_____

_____

_____

_____

_____

_____

✿SCHOOL NOTICE✿

FAILING ALERT

If you have received this notice, your grade in the following class:

_____

_____ has fallen to failing levels.

Please see your teacher immediately.

_____

_____

_____

_____

_____

_____

CITY NOTICE

An infestation of insects was found in this room. Extermination was applied. Watch for remaining bugs, especially around the bed.

STUDENT DISCIPLINE REFERRAL

 **DETENTION**

Description of infraction:

Report to the detention hall this afternoon.

You've Been Pranked!

_____

_____

_____

_____

_____

_____

OVERDUE NOTICE

Our records show that your books are overdue.

Return all checked-out
materials to the library
immediately to avoid a
hefty fine.

LIBRARY

_____

_____

_____

_____

_____

_____

❦SCHOOL NOTICE❧

FAILING ALERT

If you have received this notice, your grade in the following class:

_____

_____ has fallen to failing levels.

Please see your teacher immediately.

CITY NOTICE

An infestation of insects was found in this room. Extermination was applied. Watch for remaining bugs, especially around the bed.